Sports Illustrated KIDS

BASKETBALL'S GREATEST
MYTHS AND LEGENDS

by Elliott Smith

CAPSTONE PRESS
a capstone imprint

Published by Capstone Press, an imprint of Capstone.
1710 Roe Crest Drive, North Mankato, Minnesota 56003
capstonepub.com

Library of Congress Cataloging-in-Publication Data
Names: Smith, Elliott, 1976– author.
Title: Basketball's greatest myths and legends / by Elliott Smith.
Description: North Mankato, Minnesota : Capstone Press, [2023] | Series: Sports illustrated kids: sports greatest myths and legends | Includes bibliographical references and index. | Audience: Ages 9-11 | Audience: Grades 4-6 |
Summary: "Did Wilt Chamberlain really score 100 points by himself in a single game? Was the 1985 NBA Draft really fixed to make sure the New York Knicks got the first pick? Was Michael Jordan really let go by his high school basketball team? Get ready to discover the real stories behind these and other great basketball myths and legends!"—Provided by publisher.
Identifiers: LCCN 2022025090 (print) | LCCN 2022025091 (ebook) | ISBN 9781669003519 (hardcover) | ISBN 9781669040231 (paperback) | ISBN 9781669003472 (pdf) | ISBN 9781669003496 (kindle edition)
Subjects: LCSH: Basketball—Miscellanea—Juvenile literature. | Basketball—History—Juvenile literature. | Legends—Juvenile literature.
Classification: LCC GV885.1 .S592 2023 (print) | LCC GV885.1 (ebook) | DDC 796.323—dc23/eng/20220509
LC record available at https://lccn.loc.gov/2022025090
LC ebook record available at https://lccn.loc.gov/2022025091

Summary: Did Wilt Chamberlain really score 100 points in a single game? Was the 1985 NBA Draft really fixed to give the New York Knicks the first pick? Was Michael Jordan really let go by his high school basketball team? Discover the real stories behind these and other great basketball myths and legends!

Editorial Credits
Aaron Sautter, editor; Bobbie Nuytten, designer; Donna Metcalf, media researcher; Whitney Schaefer, production specialist

Image Credits
Alamy: agefotostock, 4; Associated Press: cover right, 15, 17, 18, Gerry Broome, 21, 23, KENNETH LAMBERT, 13, Mark Humphrey, 29, Marty Lederhandler, 28, Paul Vathis, 14; Getty Images: David E. Klutho, 5; Sports Illustrated: Andy Hayt, 25, Erick W. Rasco, cover left, 11, John W. McDonough, 19, Manny Millan, 7, 9, 28

All internet sites appearing in back matter were available and accurate when this book was sent to press.

Printed and bound in the USA. PO#5195

Table of Contents

Larger Than Life 4

The GOAT Was Cut? 6

No WNBA Dunks?.................................10

Points King.. 14

A Big Upset... 20

Lottery Tricks 24

Glossary 30

Read More....................................... 31

Internet Sites 31

Index 32

About the Author 32

Words in **bold** are in the glossary.

Larger Than Life

Basketball is huge. Millions of fans love the game. But it had small beginnings. People didn't have hoops at first. They used peach baskets!

Dr. James Naismith invented the game of basketball.

The National Basketball Association (NBA) wasn't always popular. Great players and teams helped the sport to grow. **Myths** and tall tales about them grew over time. But some myths aren't true.

Let's learn the truth behind some big basketball legends.

The GOAT Was Cut?

Michael Jordan is a legendary player. He won six NBA titles. He inspired millions of people. Some think he is the GOAT—the Greatest of All Time.

But was Jordan always a huge star? One myth says no. It says that Jordan was cut from his high school team! But that's not exactly true.

Jordan tried out for the **varsity** team. But he was a sophomore. Very few tenth graders played on varsity teams. Jordan played on the junior varsity team instead. He made varsity the next season. The rest is history.

Michael Jordan won six NBA titles with the Chicago Bulls. He also won the NBA's Most Valuable Player (MVP) award five times.

No WNBA Dunks?

The Women's National Basketball Association (WNBA) has amazing players. Yet, some people think women can't **dunk** the ball. But several players have proven that idea wrong.

Lisa Leslie played for the Los Angeles Sparks. She made the league's first dunk in 2002. She inspired the rest of the league. Since then, at least seven other women have also dunked the ball.

FACT

Brittney Griner is the WNBA dunking champ. The star **center** has 23 career dunks.

Lisa Leslie

Points King

In the early years, great players could score 40 or more points. But Wilt Chamberlain stood above them all. He often scored 60 points or more. Then on March 2, 1962, he did the unthinkable. He scored 100 points in one game!

Chamberlain set five records that day. He made 36 field goals. He added 28 free throws. And he scored the most points ever in a single game.

The Philadelphia Warriors won 169–147. It set the record for the highest-scoring game ever. The record stood for many years.

FACT

Wilt Chamberlain owns or shares four of the top five scoring games in NBA history.

Chamberlain was a great scorer. He led the NBA in scoring seven times. He later played for the Los Angeles Lakers. Chamberlain scored more than 31,000 points in his career. Many people feel that his 100-point game is an unbreakable record.

FACT

The Los Angeles Lakers' Kobe Bryant scored 81 points in a 2006 game. It was the second-highest total in history.

A Big Upset

The NCAA **tournament** is known for surprises. One of the biggest happened in 2018. The Number 16 **seed** was University of Maryland, Baltimore County. The Number 1 seed was the University of Virginia.

In 135 previous games, the Number 16 team had never beaten the Number 1 team. Not once. The games were usually blowouts. But UMBC **upset** Virginia 74–54. The Retrievers are the only #16 team to win a tournament game.

FACT

The University of Virginia Cavaliers didn't let the loss get them down. The next year, Virginia won the 2019 NCAA championship.

Lottery Tricks

For the NBA **Draft**, the worst teams are put in a **lottery**. This is meant to give them a fair chance at the best players. In 1985, Patrick Ewing was the best college player. The New York Knicks were a bad team. Ewing and the Knicks were a perfect fit.

Patrick Ewing in 1984

Many people think the 1985 lottery was fixed. They think the NBA wanted Ewing to play for the Knicks. So the league cheated.

But how? The story says that the Knicks' envelope was frozen. Then someone just picked the cold envelope. This gave the Knicks the first pick.

The Knicks did pick Ewing. And he became a Hall of Fame player. The NBA has long said that the draft wasn't **rigged**. But some fans still believe the NBA cheated.

FACT

Patrick Ewing joined the Naismith
Memorial Basketball Hall of Fame in 2008.

Glossary

center (SEN-tuhr)—one of the five positions on a basketball team; the center is often the biggest or tallest player and usually plays right under the basket

draft (DRAFT)—an event in which college athletes are picked to join a pro sports team

dunk (DUHNK)—when a player jumps above the rim and jams the ball directly into the basket

lottery (LOT-ur-ee)—a way of randomly choosing a player or team

myth (MITH)—a false idea that many people believe

rigged (RIGD)—when something is controlled to guarantee a certain outcome

seed (SEED)—how a player or team is ranked at the beginning of a tournament

tournament (TUR-nuh-muhnt)—a series of games or matches between several players or teams, ending in one winner

upset (UHP-set)—a win by a player or team that was expected to lose

varsity (VAHR-si-tee)—a first-string sports team that represents a school

Read More

Berglund, Bruce. *Basketball GOATs: The Greatest Athletes of All Time*. North Mankato, MN: Capstone Press, 2022.

Kelley, K. C. *WNBA Superstars.* Mankato, MN: The Child's World, 2020.

Levit, Joe. *Basketball's G.O.A.T.: Michael Jordan, LeBron James, and More*. Minneapolis, MN: Lerner Publications, 2020.

Internet Sites

Jr. NBA
jr.nba.com

NBA Facts for Kids
kids.kiddle.co/National_Basketball_Association

Sports Illustrated Kids: Basketball
sikids.com/basketball

Index

basketball history, 4
Bryant, Kobe, 19

Chamberlain, Wilt, 14, 16, 18
Chicago Bulls, 9

Ewing, Patrick, 24, 26, 28, 29

Griner, Brittney, 12

Hall of Fame, 28, 29

Jordan, Michael, 6, 8, 9

Leslie, Lisa, 12
Los Angeles Lakers, 18, 19
Los Angeles Sparks, 12

Most Valuable Player (MVP)
  awards, 9

National Basketball
  Association (NBA), 5, 26, 28
NBA Draft, 24, 26, 28
NBA scoring records, 14, 16,
  18, 19
NBA titles, 6, 9
NCAA tournament, 20, 22
New York Knicks, 24, 26, 28

Orlando Magic, 22

Philadelphia Warriors, 16

University of Maryland,
  Baltimore County, 20, 22
University of Virginia, 20, 22

Women's National Basketball
  Association (WNBA), 10, 12

About the Author

Elliott Smith is a former sports reporter who covered athletes in all sports from high school to the pros. He is one of the authors of the Natural Thrills series about extreme outdoor sports. In his spare time, he likes playing sports with his two children, going to the movies, and adding to his collection of Pittsburgh Steelers memorabilia.